Title Page

Healthy Lungs, Healthy Life

A Complete Guide to Breathing Better Through Nutrition, Exercise, Habits, and Mindful Living

S S Dhar

Copyright

Publisher: S S Dhar
Paperback ISBN: 978-93-5759-707-4
Hardcover ISBN: 978-93-5773-040-2
Print & Distribution: Amazon KDP

Disclaimer:

The information provided in this book is for educational and informational purposes only. It is not intended as a substitute for professional medical advice, diagnosis, or treatment. Always seek the advice of a qualified physician or healthcare provider with any questions regarding a medical condition, symptoms, or treatment options. The content presented here is based on current scientific understanding, research literature, and wellness practices at the time of writing. Individual health outcomes may vary.

Dedication

Dedicated to all those who wish to breathe freely, live consciously, and take responsibility for their health— Fresh breaths make our respiratory system healthier.
Also dedicated to those who helped me to research and complete this helpful book.

Acknowledgement

This book is the result of continuous learning, observation, and deep respect for the human body's ability to heal, adapt, and thrive.

I would like to acknowledge the countless researchers, healthcare professionals, scientists, and educators whose work in respiratory health, nutrition science, exercise physiology, and behavioral wellness has made this knowledge accessible to the world.

I would like to acknowledge the countless researchers, healthcare professionals, scientists, and educators whose work in respiratory health, nutrition science, exercise physiology, and behavioral wellness has made this knowledge accessible to the world.

I am also grateful to readers who believe that prevention is as powerful as treatment, and that small daily habits—when practiced consistently—can transform long-term health.

Finally, I acknowledge the quiet strength of the human breathing mechanism, which sustains us from the first moment of life.

— S S Dhar

Preface

Breathing is the most natural act of life—yet it is one of the most neglected. We inhale and exhale thousands of times every day without giving much thought to the lungs that make it possible. Until discomfort, disease, or breathlessness appears, lung health often remains invisible. This book was written to change that.

Healthy Lungs, Healthy Life is designed to help readers understand not only **how the lungs work**, but **how daily choices shape respiratory strength over time**. Modern life exposes our lungs to pollution, stress, poor posture, sedentary routines, and nutritional gaps. The result is a gradual decline in breathing efficiency, energy levels, and overall vitality—often without obvious warning signs.

This book bridges medical understanding with practical living. You will explore the anatomy and function of the lungs, learn how lung diseases develop, and discover how nutrition, exercise, breathing techniques, indoor air quality, and mindset directly influence respiratory health. Each chapter is structured to be clear, actionable, and relevant to everyday life.

You do not need to be ill to benefit from this book. Whether your goal is prevention, recovery, performance, or simply breathing with more ease and confidence, the principles here are meant to support you at any stage of life.

Healthy lungs are not built overnight. They are built through consistent habits, informed decisions, and mindful awareness of the breath that sustains us. My hope is that this book empowers you to take ownership of your respiratory health—and, in doing so, enhance the quality of your entire life.

Chapter No.	Table of Contents	Page no.

Chapter 1

Introduction

Healthy lungs are the unsung heroes behind every stride, every deep breath, every moment of clear thought and vitality. In ways we often take for granted, they give us the freedom to move effortlessly, stay focused at work or play, and recharge after life's challenges. This book is designed as a warm, expert companion—giving honest, practical advice rooted in science and made easy to use, so anyone can feel more confident about protecting and enhancing their respiratory health. Breathing is so much more than an unconscious act. Each breath is a meeting point where the body and mind collaborate lungs gather oxygen to fuel muscles and sharpen brain function, reinforce the heart's strength, and guard us against illness, all in one elegant rhythm. When everything is working well, energy flows freely and recovery from stress or exercise feels natural.

Discover the intricate structure of your lungs and understand their vital role in daily breathing, enhancing exercise performance, and maintaining lifelong respiratory health. Discover the intricacies of the respiratory system, exploring the journey from the nose to the alveoli. Uncover the branching airways that facilitate air delivery, the sponge-like alveolar sacs where oxygen seamlessly diffuses into the bloodstream, and the intricate capillary network responsible for transporting gases to and from every cell. Discover the diaphragm and intercostal muscles that drive every breath, explore the pleura that enables the lungs to move effortlessly, and uncover the lungs' innate defenses—mucus, cilia, surfactant, and immune sentinels—that maintain clear and adaptable airways. Connecting structure to function—ventilation, perfusion, and diffusion—reveals the reasons behind airflow constriction in asthma, the impact of alveolar damage on tolerance in COPD, the persistence of infections in various regions, and the influence of posture, air quality, and smoking on lung mechanics. By grasping the "how," you will enhance your ability to interpret symptoms, safeguard lung capacity, and make informed decisions regarding training, environment, and prevention.

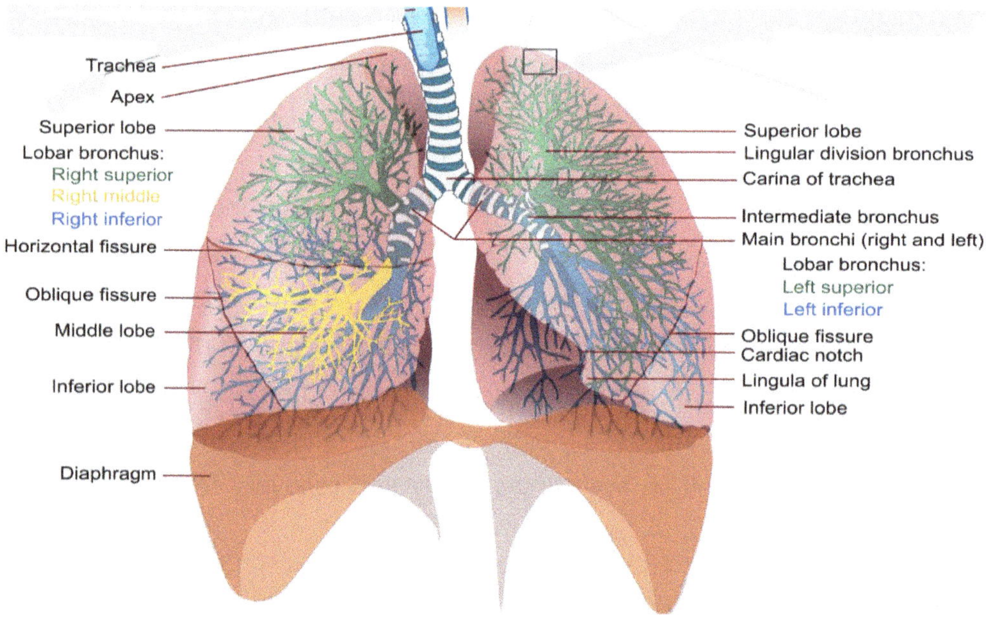

Left Lung:

The left lung contains less tissue in the anteromedial part of the organ so that the heart can fit on the left side. It consists of Superior lobs, trachea, Main Bronchi (Right, left), Inferior Lobe, Lingular division bronchus, Lingamentum. arteriosum The left lung looks different from the right lung because it has one less lobe and one less fissure. The oblique fissure of the left lung separates the organ into two parts: the superior lobe and the inferior lobe.

The inferior lobe is located posteroinferiorly relative to the oblique fissure. The superior lobe is positioned anterosuperior to the fissure. The inferior lobe is significantly larger than the superior lobe; it encompasses the majority of the left lung base, a substantial portion of the posterior border, and the lower posterior regions of both the medial and lateral surfaces. Conversely, the superior lobe encompasses the apex, the majority of the costal and medial surfaces, and the whole anterior border.

The superior lobe encompasses the cardiac notch and the corresponding lingula located in that region.

Right Lung:

The right lung is somewhat shorter and broader than the left lung. The disparities arise from the liver's position beneath the left hemidiaphragm and the heart's left-sided orientation. The right lung is larger than the left lung. Additionally, it is partitioned by two grooves into three lobes. The oblique fissure is one of two grooves present on the surface of the right lung; the other is the horizontal fissure. Both fissures partition the lung into the superior, middle, and inferior lobes.

The superior lobe of the right lung is positioned above the horizontal fissure and anteriorly superior to the oblique fissure. It encompasses the apex, the majority of the superior aspect of the costal surface, and the superior portion of the medial surface. The middle lobe is the smallest of the three lobes in the right lung. It is positioned caudally to the horizontal fissure and anteriorly to the oblique fissure. It possesses a cuneiform configuration and encompasses the anterior basal region of the lung, the anteroinferior section of the costal surface, and the inferior area of the anterior margin. The inferior lobe constitutes the predominant portion of the lung surface volume. It is located posterior to the oblique fissure. This lobe comprises the posteroinferior regions of the costal and medial surfaces, as well as the complete lung base located posterior to the oblique fissure.

Trachea:

The tracheobronchial tree is made up of the trachea and bronchi. At the tracheal bifurcation, the thoracic portion splits into the left and right major bronchi. The carina is a sagittally orientated cartilaginous ridge located in the tracheal bifurcation.

In comparison to the left, the right major bronchus is shorter, broader, and runs nearly vertically. As a result, it is more vulnerable to blockages by foreign bodies. The lungs are supplied by progressively smaller intrapulmonary bronchi that split out from each main bronchus.

Air is transported to the pulmonary lobes by lobar bronchi. For the three lobes of the right lung, the right main bronchus divides into superior, middle, and inferior lobar bronchi. For the two lobes of the left lung, the left main bronchus then splits into superior and inferior lobar bronchi.

The bronchopulmonary segments are aerated by segmental bronchi. Ten to twelve segmental bronchi, one for each bronchopulmonary segment, are formed by the division of the three lobar bronchi on the right side. The two lobar bronchi on the left side also split off to form eight to ten segmental bronchi.

Air is transported even deeper into the bronchopulmonary segments by intra-tegmental (subsegmental) bronchi. There are roughly fifteen intra-segmental bronchi for every segmental bronchi. The pulmonary lobules and alveoli are the end result of numerous bronchioles that are released by the intra-segmental bronchi.

The respiratory system's conducting zone includes the bronchioles. Air can go from the trachea into the alveoli, where gaseous exchange takes place, thanks to the conducting zone.

Initially, the bronchioles are bronchi. From the trachea, the left and right major bronchi emerge into the lungs. They then split off into even smaller bronchi. The branches that extend past the terminal segmental bronchi are known as bronchioles. The number of bronchiole branches can range from 20 to 25.

Bronchioles come in two varieties:

Air is conducted by conducting bronchioles, which do not have glands or alveoli. In addition to conducting air, respiratory bronchioles have alveoli that protrude from their lumens. The lungs' fundamental unit for gas exchange is the alveoli. Alveolar ducts emerge from these bronchioles, and alveolar sacs follow. There are cartilage plates in the bronchi. But the passageways get smaller when they split off into bronchioles. This indicates that the walls of bronchioles lack cartilage plates. Rather, bronchioles are bordered by cuboidal epithelium and include a substantial layer of smooth muscle within their walls.

Chapter 2

Understanding the Lung System

Overview:

The lungs are paired, cone-shaped organs in the thoracic cavity on either side of the heart, designed to bring oxygen into the blood and remove carbon dioxide. Their architecture balances a large surface area with thin barriers to allow maximum expansion and flexibility for effortless ventilation.

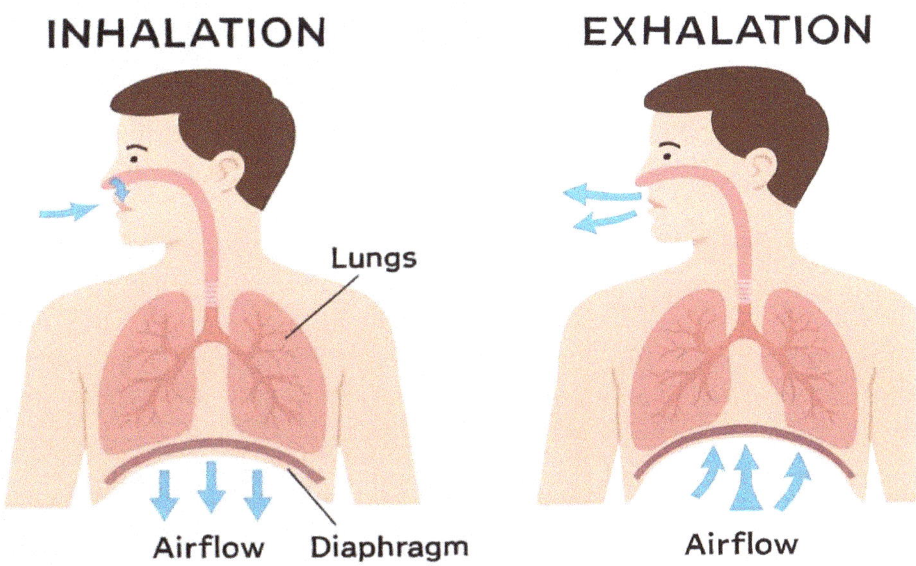

Lobes and fissures:

The right lung has three lobes separated by horizontal and oblique fissures, while the left lung has two lobes separated by a transverse fissure and a cardiac notch that encloses the heart. The lobes are further divided into bronchopulmonary segments, clinically useful units that can be separated during disease or surgery.

1. *How Breathing Works:*

Airway tree:

Air flows into the body via the nasal cavity and pharynx, moving through the larynx and trachea before splitting into the right and left main bronchi, which further divide into lobar and segmental bronchi. The bronchi progressively narrow and divide into bronchioles and terminal bronchioles, forming a remarkably efficient network for distributing airflow.

Respiratory zone:

The terminal bronchioles transition into respiratory bronchioles, leading to alveolar ducts and alveolar sacs, which together form the acinus, the site of gas exchange. This transition signifies the change from air conduction to diffusion through very thin membranes.

Alveoli and cells:

- Alveoli are tiny, sponge-like sacs that provide a vast surface area for the diffusion of gases. Type I pneumocytes form the thin diffusion barrier, while Type II pneumocytes secrete surfactant to reduce surface tension and prevent alveolar collapse. A typical adult has 300 million to 500 million alveoli.

Cavity and Pleura:

A thin fluid-filled pleural cavity that permits frictionless gliding during breathing is surrounded by a double-layered pleura, with the parietal layer on the chest wall and the visceral layer on the lung. The lungs are kept expanded against the chest wall by the negative pressure in this area.

The flow and supply of blood:

Pulmonary veins return oxygenated blood to the heart, while pulmonary arteries transport deoxygenated blood to alveolar capillaries for gas exchange. While extensive lymphatics support fluid balance and immune surveillance, bronchial arteries supply airway tissues with nutrient-rich blood.

Breathing muscles: With the help of external intercostals, the diaphragm, the main muscle of inspiration, flattens downward to increase the thoracic volume; at rest, expiration is primarily passive recoil. The sternocleidomastoid, scalene, internal intercostals, and abdominal wall are accessory muscles that enhance ventilation during exertion or respiratory distress.

Elasticity and mechanics:

Elastic fibers and collagen within lung parenchyma provide compliance for easy inflation and elastic recoil for efficient exhalation. Uniform ventilation depends on airway caliber, surfactant function, and the integrity of inter-alveolar connections such as pores of Kohn.

Defenses of the airways:

While ciliated epithelium propels the mucociliary escalator in the direction of the pharynx, mucus traps particles. Macrophages, dendritic cells, and lymphocytes are examples of innate and adaptive immune sentinels that patrol the interstitial space and airways to neutralize pathogens.

Nervous regulation:

Airway tone and glandular secretion are regulated by autonomic innervation; sympathetic pathways encourage bronchodilation, whereas parasympathetic activity tends to narrow airways and produce more mucus. Breathing patterns and reflexes like coughing are controlled by stretch and irritant receptors.

Chapter 3

Root causes: How Lung problems begin

The Magnitude of the Problem

Lung cancer remains one of the most significant public health challenges worldwide, ranking as the leading cause of cancer mortality. In 2025, over 226,000 new cases are expected to be diagnosed in the U.S. alone, representing approximately 11% of all new cancer cases, with more than 124,000 projected deaths (about 20% of all cancer deaths). Globally, lung cancer accounted for about 2.5 million new cases in 2022. The 5-year survival rate remains low at about 28%, underscoring both the deadliness and urgency of prevention and early detection.

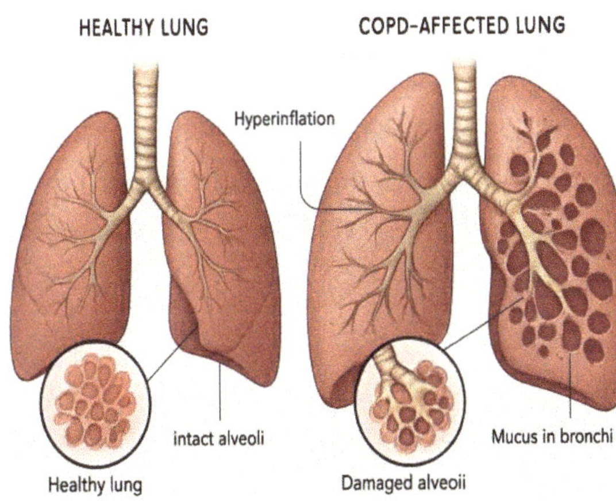

Environmental drivers

Outdoor air pollution is a significant contributor to respiratory disease globally, which the likelihood of developing COPD, lung cancer, and infections rises significantly; nearly the entire global population is exposed to air quality that exceeds recommended limits, with the most severe impact felt in low- and middle-income nations. The impact of climate change manifests in the form of wildfires, dust storms, and stagnant air, creating an environment that traps pollutants and adversely affects lung health across all age groups.

- Environmental pollution, such as fine particles and ozone, damages the airways, reduces lung function, and greatly shortens life expectancy, leading to increased hospitalizations for asthma, COPD, and respiratory infections.

- Occupational exposure to silica and asbestos are naturally occurring minerals, but they have distinct properties and health effects. While both can cause lung disease, silica dust is increasingly recognized as a significant workplace hazard, sometimes referred to as the "new asbestos" because of its potential for serious respiratory illness with prolonged exposure.
- Another harmful indoor natural radioactive gas, radon, is the second leading cause of lung cancer and the leading cause in nonsmokers, and smoking and poor ventilation in basements increase the risk.

Damp, moldy housing increases the risk of respiratory symptoms, shortness of breath, asthma, and infections in the pulmonary system; remediation focuses on humidity control, ventilation, and removal of persistent dampness and visible mold.

Lifestyle choices:

Smoking is the most common cause of lung disease that can be avoided. It is the main cause of COPD (chronic obstructive pulmonary disease) fatalities, makes asthma worse, raises the risk of TB and pneumonia, and slows lung expansion in young people. Secondhand smoke causes respiratory problems and diseases in both children and adults. Quitting smoking at any age makes symptoms better, slows down the decline, and lowers the risk of cancer and infections. Smoking (both active and passive) hurts the airways and alveoli, which can lead to COPD (chronic obstructive pulmonary disease) and a higher risk of infections and numerous respiratory symptoms. Quitting smoking quickly and for good helps your lungs.

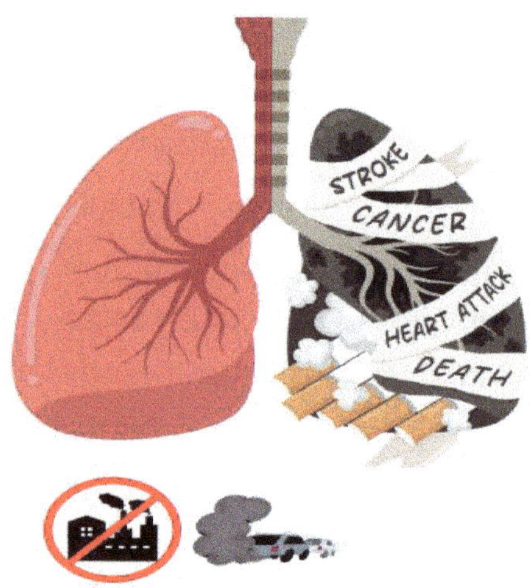

Pic shows : Lifestyle choices effect lung health

Vaping can trigger EVALI (e-cigarette, or vaping, product-associated lung injury), an acute, sometimes fatal lung injury linked to chemicals such as vitamin

E acetate and other ingredients in THC (delta-9-tetrahydrocannabinol) products; symptoms include shortness of breath, cough, chest pain, fever, and GI upset (gastrointestinal upset). A high BMI is associated with an increased risk of asthma and chronic disease, while being overweight worsens shortness of breath and exercise tolerance, highlighting the role of weight control in respiratory health. Some of these benefits include weight loss.

Early Warning Indications:

A persistent or worsening cough that occurs daily, shortness of breath during physical activity or at work, sporadic chest tightness, frequent "chest colds," or changes in sputum should all be assessed and spirometry should be done.

Spirometry:

Spirometry is a simple, non-invasive pulmonary function test that measures how much and how quickly you can move air in and out of your lungs. Healthcare professionals use it to diagnose and monitor lung conditions such as asthma and COPD (chronic obstructive pulmonary disease), helping to assess lung strength and the effectiveness of treatment.

Exposure can cause lung inflammation. Polluted air, cold air, or irritants can worsen cough, mucus, and shortness of breath for days to weeks in the case of chronic lung conditions.

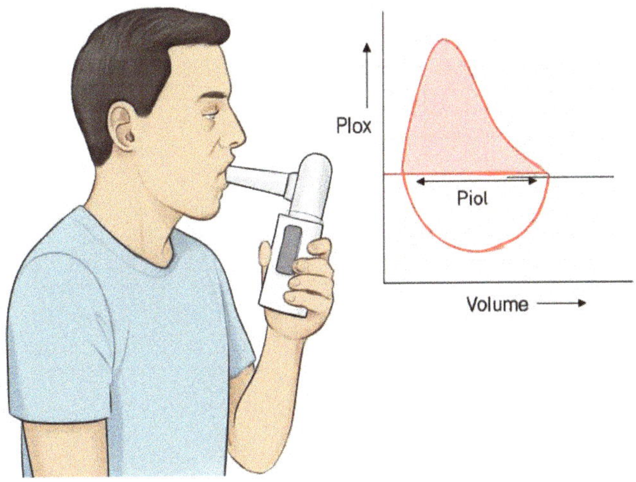

Common early symptoms:

Shortness of breath (especially with activity), wheezing, chronic cough (often with mucus), chest tightness, and recurrent respiratory infections.

Related changes: Increased frequency of coughing, thick or discolored mucus, fever with chest symptoms, or decreased exercise capacity compared to baseline.

Emergency symptoms:

Severe shortness of breath, blue lips or fingernails, chest pain, or confusion; these conditions require immediate emergency care. By addressing some of these key factors and acting on early warning signs in our daily lives, it is possible to meaningfully reduce the risk of chronic and acute lung diseases and preserve long-term respiratory health. In research, the researcher found that the average healthy person could hold their breath for 45 to 50 seconds, while patients with weak heart muscles could do so but for only 10 to 20 seconds.

Chapter 4

Types of Lung Diseases:

Any issue affecting the lungs that hinders their normal function is referred to as lung disease. Lung diseases can be divided into three categories:

Airway Diseases : The tubes (airways) that transport oxygen and other gases into and out of the lungs are impacted by airway illnesses. The airways typically constrict or become blocked as a result of them. Asthma, bronchiolitis, chronic obstructive pulmonary disease (COPD), and bronchiectasis—the primary condition affecting people with cystic fibrosis—are examples of airway illnesses. Individuals who suffer from airway disorders frequently describe feeling as though they are "trying to breathe out through a straw."

Lung tissue Diseases: These conditions impact the lung tissue's structure. The lungs cannot fully expand due to tissue scarring or inflammation (restrictive lung disease). The lungs have a harder time absorbing oxygen and exhaling carbon dioxide as a result. Individuals who suffer from this kind of lung condition frequently describe feeling as though they are "wearing a too-tight sweater or vest." They are unable to breathe deeply as a result. Lung tissue diseases include sarcoidosis and pulmonary fibrosis.

Lung circulation Disorders: These conditions impact the lungs' blood vessels. They are brought on by blood vessel irritation, scarring, or clotting. They have an impact on the lungs' capacity to absorb oxygen and expel carbon dioxide. Heart function may also be impacted by certain conditions. Pulmonary hypertension is one example of a lung circulation illness. When they exert themselves, people with these diseases frequently experience severe dyspnea.

The most common lung diseases include: Asthma, Collapse of part or all of the lung (pneumothorax or atelectasis), Swelling and inflammation in the main passages (bronchial tubes) that carry air to the lungs (bronchitis),

COPD (Chronic obstructive pulmonary disease), Lung cancer, Lung infection (pneumonia).

COPD (*Chronic obstructive pulmonary disease),*

The prevalent lung condition known as chronic obstructive pulmonary disease (COPD) results in breathing difficulties and reduced airflow. It is occasionally referred to as chronic bronchitis or emphysema.

People with COPD may experience lung damage or phlegm blockage. Symptoms include fatigue, wheezing, breathing difficulties, and coughing, occasionally with phlegm.

The most prevalent causes of COPD are air pollution and smoking. Other health issues are more likely to affect people with COPD.

Although there is no cure for COPD, symptoms can be lessened if a person gets vaccinated against illnesses and abstains from smoking and air pollution. Additionally, medications, oxygen, and pulmonary rehabilitation can be used to treat it.

Reasons of COPD:

COPD can result from a number of factors that constrict the airways. The airway lining may be inflamed and swollen, mucus may obstruct the airways, and portions of the lung may be destroyed.

Over time, COPD develops gradually and is frequently caused by a combination of risk factors:

In low- and middle-income countries with high levels of smoke exposure, biomass fuel (wood, animal dung, crop residue) or coal is commonly used for cooking and heating; early life events like poor growth in utero, prematurity, and frequent or severe respiratory infections in childhood that prevent maximum lung growth; childhood asthma; occupational exposure to dusts, fumes, or chemicals; indoor air pollution; and a rare genetic condition called alpha-1 antitrypsin deficiency, which can cause COPD at an early age.

If a person exhibits common symptoms, they should be suspected of having COPD. A breathing test called spirometry, which gauges lung function, can confirm the diagnosis. Since spirometry is frequently unavailable in low- and middle-income nations, the diagnosis may go unnoticed.

Chapter 5

The hidden effects of unhealthy lungs

Unhealthy lungs silently impair physical performance, increase the risk of heart disease, and create a major economic burden—often years before a formal diagnosis is made or symptoms are recognized as having a respiratory origin. These effects are driven by reduced oxygen delivery, systemic inflammation, and exposure-driven injury (such as air pollution), and these spill over into energy levels, cardiovascular health, and family and national finances.

Physical Performance:

Even modest chronic lung disease makes it harder to breathe and lowers cardiorespiratory fitness. This makes people tired more quickly, takes longer to recover, and makes them less able to do everyday tasks and exercise. In COPD, skeletal muscle dysfunction—characterized by diminished oxidative capacity, abnormalities in fiber type, and modifications in mitochondrial function—serves as a principal factor contributing to exercise limitation and fatigue, irrespective of spirometric assessments.

Chronic hypoxemia and systemic inflammation hasten muscle atrophy and fatigue, resulting in deconditioning and diminished VO2max, despite seemingly minor declines in lung function. Sarcopenia is prevalent in chronic lung disease; in COPD, the aggregated prevalence nears 29%, reducing mobility, balance, and strength, and further diminishing activity levels. As oxygen levels drop, cognitive stress and "brain fog" might get worse. Chronic hypoxemia and inflammation make it harder to pay attention and remember things, which makes studying and working harder.

Cardiovascular consequences:

If you have bad lungs, it can make heart disease worse by causing pulmonary hypertension, low oxygen levels, arrhythmias (irregular heartbeats), and making chronic heart disease worse. There is a strong link between lung disease and the heart. After COPD gets worse, the risk of acute coronary syndrome, stroke, arrhythmia, heart failure, or mortality goes up and stays high for months. This shows how airway inflammation and hypoxemia can affect the whole body. Air pollution, a respiratory toxin, is a major cause of heart disease deaths worldwide. Most pollution-related deaths happen through pathways like endothelial dysfunction, thrombosis, and autonomic imbalance that led to ischemic heart disease and stroke.

After a COPD flare-up, the risk of significant heart disease is highest in the first week (more than ten times higher) and rises over the next 6 to 12 months, showing that the heart is still under stress. Heart attacks and strokes are significantly linked to exposure to PM 2.5 in the air; heart disease is responsible for over 70% of deaths from outdoor air pollution worldwide, showing how exposure to the "lungs" hurts the heart. Medical statistics say that if nothing is done to improve air quality, heart disease and fatalities caused by pollution will rise, especially in South and East Asia.

Economic burden:

Poor lung health drains household finances and national economies through increased medical costs, reduced productivity, and alarming increases for low- income households. In low- and middle-income countries, the societal cost of COPD per patient is in the hundreds of thousands of dollars and includes hospitalizations, medications, oxygen, and significant income loss, with wide variation across countries and access to care. In many countries, air pollution-related illnesses (mostly respiratory and cardiovascular) cost an estimated 1.36% of GDP in 2019 through premature deaths and lost productivity due to illness, with a more severe burden in low- income states.

Business-focused analyses estimate that absenteeism, attendance, and reduced consumer activity from polluted air cost U.S. companies hundreds of billions of dollars annually, a recurring blow comparable to a large macroeconomic shock. At the macro level, air pollution measurably slows annual GDP growth in many countries, showing that unhealthy air weakens both lungs and economic resilience.

Emotional and cognitive impairment:

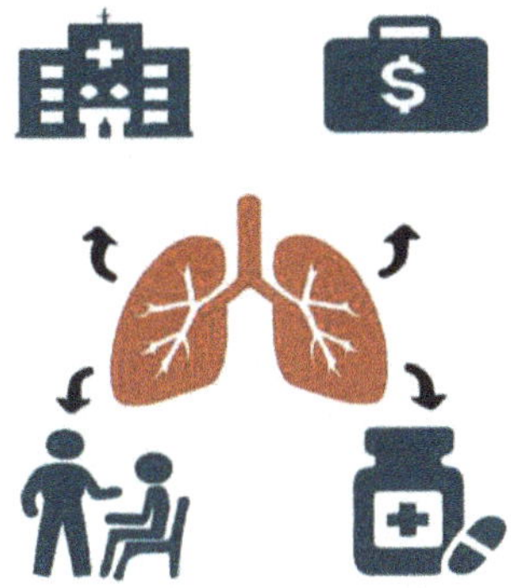

Pic Shows :Economic Burden of Poor Lung Health

Depression and anxiety are significantly more common in chronic lung disease and independently worsen symptoms, hospitalizations, and costs, creating a feedback loop of poor adherence and higher utilization. COPD is also associated with a higher risk of cognitive impairment through chronic hypoxemia and systemic inflammation, which complicates self-management and daily functioning. The estimated prevalence of depression in COPD is about one- quarter worldwide, with anxiety often co-occurring and associated with more exacerbations and longer hospital stays. Hypoxemia and inflammatory mediators disrupt cerebrovascular and nervous system integrity, contributing to measurable deficits in memory and attention that affect work and quality of life.

Why it stays secret:

Early signs of limitations are small, like skipping stairs, taking shorter walks, or having "low energy days." These are often mistaken for aging or stress as deconditioning and muscle changes build up before lung tests "look bad." External factors like PM 2.5 can put stress on the cardiovascular system, so the first clear sign of a problem might be a heart issue instead of a lung problem, which makes it harder to see where the risk comes from.

What helps:

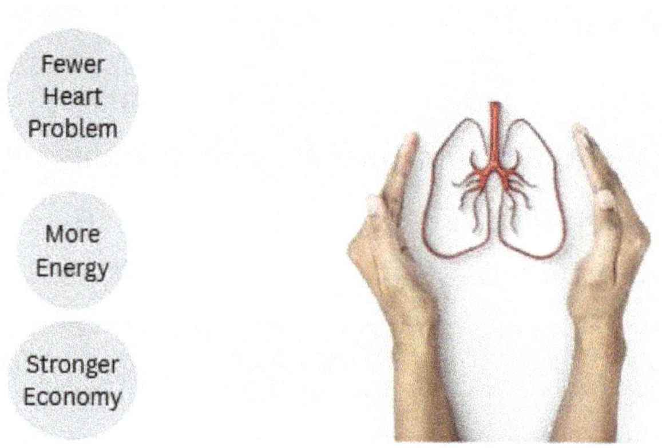

Pulmonary rehabilitation and regular endurance and resistance training can help with VO2max, strength, symptoms, and daily function. They can also help with systemic deconditioning. Cleaner air policies are good for both health and the economy because they lower the risk of heart and lung disease in the whole population. Screening and treating depression and anxiety in people with chronic lung disease can help them have fewer flare-ups, shorter hospital stays, and lower overall healthcare costs. This can lead to better adherence and outcomes.

These hidden effects show why protecting lung health has many benefits, such as more energy and productivity, fewer heart problems, and stronger economies at home and in the country.

Chapter 6

The Ripple effect: Benefits of Healthy Lungs

Healthy lungs create a foundation for optimal oxygen delivery and sustained energy by efficiently transferring oxygen from air to blood, enabling cellular ATP production, and supporting peak physical and cognitive performance across all life stages. The benefits ripple through everybody system—from superior exercise capacity and mental clarity to enhanced recovery and longevity.

Benefits for athletic performance:

Higher lung function translates directly into increased exercise capacity and endurance performance. Elite athletes have significantly higher VO_2max values — up to 60+ mL/kg/min in men, compared to 33 mL/kg/min during sedentary exercise—reflecting their lungs' superior ability to deliver oxygen during peak exertion. Across a range of athletes, lung function parameters, including vital capacity, forced expiratory volume, and maximal voluntary ventilation, are increased, with endurance sports providing the greatest respiratory adaptations compared to sedentary individuals. Respiratory muscle training can improve breathing and respiratory effort by 15-30%, reducing perceived exertion and delaying fatigue during high-intensity exercise, especially beneficial for those who rely heavily on sustained oxygen delivery. Even in older athletes, lung capacity remains superior to that of sedentary peers, although it still declines with age; this suggests that maintaining lung health through activity preserves respiratory benefits throughout life.

Pic shows: Enabling cellular ATP production and Peak Physical Performance

Every day energy and vitality

Healthy lungs support consistent energy levels during daily activities, ensuring efficient oxygen delivery to all tissues, preventing fatigue and shortness of breath that characterizes respiratory problems. Regular deep breathing exercises and physical activity increase lung capacity utilization from 50% to full capacity at rest. Diaphragmatic breathing techniques can improve oxygen efficiency and reduce respiratory energy expenditure, freeing up metabolic resources for other activities and increasing overall vitality. Higher levels of physical activity are also associated with slower declines in lung function in conditions such as asthma, with active individuals preserving FEV and overall respiratory capacity compared to sedentary peers. Proper hydration helps maintain thin mucus secretions, reduces airway resistance, and supports respiratory function, which conserves energy for other activities. Breathing techniques that optimize oxygen utilization can increase mitochondrial density and cristae formation, improve the cell's aerobic energy production capacity, and reduce oxidative stress. Mind-body breathing practices can activate nitric oxide pathways that improve both pulmonary gas exchange and mitochondrial oxygen utilization, creating synergistic benefits for cellular energy metabolism. Improved oxygen supply supports electron transport chain function, enabling more efficient ATP synthesis and reducing the production of harmful reactive oxygen species that can damage cellular components.

Oxygen Delivery and Energy:

Healthy lungs maintain mental clarity and emotional balance through optimal oxygen delivery to the brain, activation of the parasympathetic nervous system through controlled breathing, and neurochemical changes that increase focus, reduce anxiety, and enhance emotional stability. The brain's high oxygen demand—consuming 20% of the body's total oxygen even though it is only 2% of body weight—makes efficient pulmonary function critical for cognitive performance and mental well-being.

Oxygen and brain function:

- The brain's high metabolic demands require consistent oxygen delivery through efficient pulmonary gas exchange to maintain cellular energy production and prevent cognitive decline.

- Hypoxia affects multiple cognitive domains, including attention span, short- term memory, complex thinking, and decision-making, with severity correlating to the duration and degree of oxygen reduction.
- Chronic oxygen deficits can lead to structural brain changes, including hippocampus and cortex atrophy, alpha-synuclein protein aggregation, and neurodegeneration that may become irreversible.
- Enhanced oxygen delivery through healthy lung function supports neuroplasticity, angiogenesis, and synaptic plasticity—processes crucial for learning, memory, and adaptation.

Cognitive Performance Benefits

- Breathing exercises such as pranayama and yoga increase the ability to focus, reduce mind wandering, improve arousal levels, and increase cognitive flexibility.
- Alternate nostril breathing (annuloma-viloma) helps balance the left and right hemispheres of the brain, increasing mental clarity, improving concentration, and improving overall cognitive integration.
- Oxygen supplementation studies show that a small increase in oxygen concentration (35% compared to room air) can significantly improve verbal memory and alter brain wave patterns associated with improved cognitive performance.
- Regular breathing exercises can improve working memory, attention span, and problem-solving abilities by directing blood flow and oxygen to the prefrontal cortex region, which is important for performance.

Mental Clarity and Emotional Balance:

Controlled breathing activities engage different physiological and psychological mechanisms that increase mental balance and resilience to stress. These methods work by activating the parasympathetic nervous system, thereby lowering cortisol levels, and causing measurable changes in brain areas that are linked to emotional processing.

- Deep breathing exercises like 4-7-8 breathing start the body's relaxation response, which breaks the cycle of ongoing stress that can cause anxiety, depression, and erratic emotions.

- Box breathing and diaphragmatic breathing help control heart rate, lower blood pressure, ease muscle tension, and change brain waves from a high-alert state to a calmer, more focused state.
- Studies show that breathing interventions work best when they don't go too fast, last at least 5 minutes, have a human guide, and have multiple sessions with long-term practice.
- Hyperbaric oxygen therapy (HBOT) may help with symptoms of PTSD, anxiety, and depression by making the brain more flexible, lowering inflammation, and speeding up healing in areas of the brain that control emotions.

Benefits for long-term brain health:

Breathing exercises done regularly and keeping the lungs working well lead to permanent changes in the brain's structure and function that help keep your mind strong and your emotions stable for the rest of your life. These benefits encompass enhanced neuroplasticity, augmented stress resilience, and safeguarding against cognitive deterioration associated with aging.

Regular meditation and controlled breathing exercises enhance cortical thickness, diminish amygdala reactivity, and augment overall brain connectivity, resulting in improved emotional regulation and cognitive performance.

Enriched oxygen therapy has been demonstrated to ameliorate age-related cognitive decline by enhancing autophagy, diminishing tau hyperphosphorylation, and facilitating synaptic organization in the aging brain. It is a medical treatment involving delivering higher-than-normal concentrations of oxygen to the body to treat various conditions,

Physical and mental activities that enhance optimal oxygen circulation to the brain may avert the development of hypoxic regions and facilitate angiogenesis, potentially aiding in the preservation of cognitive function throughout one's lifetime.

Intermittent hypoxic preconditioning—regulated exposure to mild oxygen deprivation succeeded by recovery—may augment the brain's resilience to subsequent challenges and improve neuroprotection.

Chapter 7

Power Fruits: Most Effective Fruits for Healthy Lung

Consuming fruits that are high in antioxidants and anti-inflammatories is a good way to keep your lungs healthy. These fruits help your lungs work better, boost your immune system, and fight oxidative stress. This is a complete guide to the best fruits for lung health, including who can eat them, how much they should eat, when they should eat them, and how to pair them with other foods. It also talks about the benefits of these fruits for lung patients.

1. The Best Fruits for Lung Support:

Fruit Names	Key Nutrients	Benefits
Berries (blue, strawberries, raspberries)	Vitamin C, quercetin, anthocyanins	Neutralize free radicals; reduce airway inflammation;
Citrus (oranges, lemons, grapefruit)	Vitamin C, flavonoids	Enhance collagen synthesis in lung tissue; support
Apples	Quercetin, fiber	Improve lung function; slow age-related decline; modulate
Pomegranates	Polyphenols, vitamin C	Reduce mucus production; improve oxygen uptake
Kiwi	Vitamins C & E, folate	Strengthen epithelial barriers; support cilia function

Papaya	Vitamin A precursors, antioxidants	Support mucosal health; protect against pollutants
Avocado	Vitamin E, monounsaturated fats	Defend cell membranes; reduce systemic inflammation
Watermelon	Lycopene, citrulline	Enhance nitric oxide production; improve vascular

2. Adults Who Can Eat and Suggested Amounts:

Berries: 1 cup per day,
Apples: 1 small to medium whole fruit per weekday.
Pomegranate: ½ cup arils per day.
Kiwi/Papaya: 1 fruit or 1 cup cubed per
day. Avocado: ¼ to ½ fruit per day.
Watermelon: 1 cup cubed per day.

Children older than three years:

Berries: half a cup every day
Adjusted citrus/applicable size: ½ cup juice or ½ fruit

- Watermelon: ½ cup cubed daily
- Avocado: 2 tablespoons daily
- Kiwi/Papaya: ½ fruit or ½ cup cubed twice weekly
- Apples: ½ small fruit daily

Apple

Berries

Pomogrenade

Avacado

Watermelon

Kiwi

3. Who Should Avoid or Limit

✓ Fructose intolerance or fructose malabsorption: Limit high-sugar fruits (mango, watermelon) and monitor symptoms.

✓ Gastroesophageal reflux disease (GERD): Avoid acidic fruits on an empty stomach (citrus, pineapple).

✓ Kidney stones or hyperkalemia: Consume high-potassium fruits (avocado, kiwi, orange) in moderation and under medical guidance.

✓ Pollen-related oral allergy syndrome: Peel skins or cook apples/kiwi to reduce allergenicity for susceptible individuals.

4. Fruits and Nuts as a Pairing for Equilibrium Energy

Nuts and fruits together add good fats, stabilize blood sugar, and give you long-lasting energy:

1. Almonds and Berries
2. Slices of apple plus halves of walnut
3. Pistachios and Kiwi
4. Cashews plus orange segments
5. Brazil nuts plus chunks of papaya

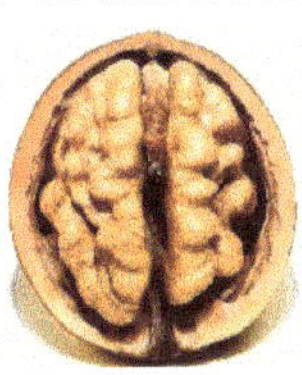
Walnut

Berries

Almonds

Apple

Aim for a 1:1 by volume ratio (¼ cup fruit to ¼ cup nuts) as a pre-workout or afternoon snack.

5. Advice for the Seasons

✓ **Spring:** kiwis, berries (peak strawberry season)
✓ **Summertime:** avocado, watermelon, papaya, and citrus (late flush)
✓ **Autumn:** Apples, pomegranates, and citrus (early harvest) in the fall
✓ **Winter:** Avocado, pomegranate, and citrus (grapefruit, orange).

Consuming fruits when they are in season guarantees the best possible nutrient density, taste, and cost.

6. Advantages for the Lung:

Antioxidant defense in patients lowers inflammation and oxidative stress in the airways.

- Vitamins C and E promote mucosal integrity and the synthesis of surfactants.
- Polyphenols and flavonoids lower the risk of infection and regulate immune responses.
- Fruits like watermelon provide hydration, which thins mucus.
- Fiber promotes the health of the gut microbiota, which affects lung immunity and systemic inflammation.

7. Best timing to eat:

- **Post-flare or exacerbation:** Begin with gentle fruits (ripe banana, melon) to ease digestion.
- **Stable periods:** Incorporate full range of power fruits daily as tolerated.
- **During rehabilitation:** Pair fruit + nut snack 30–60 minutes before pulmonary rehabilitation sessions to sustain energy.

8. Best Time to Eat Daily Basis:

- Morning: Citrus or kiwi to jump-start antioxidant support and energy.
- Mid-morning snack: Berries + nuts to curb cravings and stabilize blood sugar.
- Pre-exercise/rehabilitation: Apple + almonds for sustained energy and hydration.
- Afternoon: Papaya or pomegranate to combat post-lunch fatigue.
- Evening: Avocado slices or small fruit portions to support overnight repair without reflux.

Fruits with high water content, like watermelons, contribute to overall hydration and help keep mucus from becoming thick in the airways. This fruit can help with lung detoxification and improve breathing. By integrating these power fruits into balanced, seasonal, and well-timed eating habits—while tailoring choices to individual tolerances—adults and children alike can harness natural nutrients to fortify lung health, boost energy, and complement medical or rehabilitative strategies.

Chapter 8

Power Foods: Most effective foods for lung health

Foods that protect lung health center on anti-inflammatory, antioxidant, and microbiome-supporting patterns such as Mediterranean/DASH-style eating, omega-3–rich foods, high-fiber plants, nitrate-rich vegetables, green tea, and

fermented dairy, which together support oxygen delivery, exercise capacity, and infection resistance across ages. Practical timing add-ons like nitrate-rich beetroot before rehab and avoiding caffeine before spirometry can fine-tune performance and testing accuracy for people with lung conditions.

1. What to eat:

Fatty Fish

Chia Seed

Beetroot

Spinach

Green Tea

- Mediterranean/DASH pattern: vegetables, legumes, whole grains, nuts, olive oil, and fish are associated with better spirometry profiles, fewer symptoms, and lower COPD prevalence in observational data.

- Omega-3 foods: fatty fish, flaxseed, chia, and walnuts align with evidence linking higher circulating EPA/DHA to lower COPD morbidity and slower lung function decline, though RCTs show mixed functional endpoints with reduced IL-6 inflammation.

- Nitrate-rich vegetables: beetroot, spinach, rocket, and leafy greens can enhance endothelial function and exercise endurance; acute beetroot juice improved shuttle-walk endurance in COPD requiring oxygen.

- High-fiber foods: whole grains, legumes, vegetables, and fruit drive short-chain fatty acids that modulate airway inflammation via the gut–lung axis, with experimental and translational evidence showing suppressed allergic airway inflammation.

- Green tea: Catechin-rich extracts reduce oxidative stress and Th2 cytokines in experimental airway inflammation, supporting a role for tea polyphenols alongside standard care.
- Fermented dairy/probiotics: yogurt/kefir with live cultures reduce incidence and duration of acute upper respiratory infections and antibiotic use in meta-analyses.

- Coffee (caffeine): modest, short-lived bronchodilation occurs for up to 4 hours, which can confound spirometry results if consumed beforehand.

2.Limit processed meats:

Higher processed meat intake is prospectively linked to greater COPD risk, especially among ever-smokers and those with lower diet quality.

3.Who should avoid or limit:

- Avoid caffeine within 4 hours before spirometry because it causes measurable bronchodilation that can alter test interpretation.
- Processed meats should be minimized due to prospective links with higher COPD risk, particularly in smokers and low-quality diets.

- Vitamin D supplementation should be individualized and clinician-guided (especially in deficiency), with daily or weekly dosing showing ARI protection rather than intermittent bolus.

4.Pairing tips (balanced energy):

- Combine high-fiber plants with olive oil or nuts and a protein source in Mediterranean/DASH-style meals (e.g., chickpeas + leafy greens + olive oil; whole grains + walnuts + vegetables) to reinforce anti-inflammatory and antioxidant patterns associated with better lung metrics.
- Before rehab or walks, pair a nitrate-rich veg option (e.g., beetroot salad) with a Mediterranean-style meal to support acute endurance and vascular responses documented with beetroot dosing.

5.When can a lung patient eat:

- Stable phases: use Mediterranean/DASH daily, layer in omega-3s, fiber, probiotics, green tea, and nitrate-rich vegetables to support symptoms and resilience based on the above associations and trials.
- Pre-rehabilitation or exertion: consider nitrate-rich options (e.g., beetroot) prior to sessions to leverage documented acute endurance gains in COPD.
- Testing days: avoid caffeine within ~4 hours before spirometry to prevent test confounding from bronchodilation.

6.Best time to eat:

- Consistency beats clock time for Mediterranean/DASH, fiber, probiotics, and green tea; prioritize daily inclusion to mirror the habitual patterns linked with better lung outcomes. Time nitrate-rich foods/beetroot closer to activity or rehab sessions when acute endurance benefits are most relevant in COPD phenotypes studied.

- Schedule caffeine away from lung function testing windows due to its measurable, short-term broncho dilatory effects.

Note: Vitamin D is most beneficial when dosed daily or weekly—especially in those with low baseline levels—and should be coordinated with a clinician as part of respiratory infection prevention and overall respiratory health planning.

Chapter 9

Effective Juice: Most effective Juices for Healthy Lung

When it comes to lung health, the most effective juices are those that are rich in vegetables, antioxidants, and nitrates. Beetroot, tomato, and pomegranate juice, which are rich in polyphenols, are particularly beneficial. These juices should be consumed regularly with meals and, for optimal performance, should be timed before activity. This will help support oxygen delivery, airway inflammation control, and exercise capacity. Because whole-diet patterns continue to be the most important, juices are most effective when they are added as targeted additions to a Mediterranean or DASH-style diet, which is associated with improved spirometry and less respiratory symptoms.

1. ### The most powerful juices are:

   Extract of beetroot: Beetroot, which is rich in nitrates, has been shown to increase plasma nitrate and nitrite levels and to enhance walking endurance and shuttle-walk performance in patients with chronic obstructive pulmonary disease (COPD). This is especially true when the beetroot is consumed prior to or in conjunction with pulmonary rehabilitation. However, some investigations have reported that it has no effect on performance.

   Lycopene-rich tomato juice: which delivered around 45 milligrams of lycopene per day, was found to reduce inflammation in the airways of neutrophils and enhance asthma control markers in a proof-of-concept trial that was conducted in a crossover fashion.

   Pomegranate juice and extract: Pomegranate extract improved asthma symptoms and enhanced FEV1/FVC-related parameters in mild–moderate asthma, with animal and mechanistic data supporting anti-inflammatory and antifibrotic potential; juice provides similar polyphenols, albeit at lower, food-level doses. Pomegranate juice and extract are both sources of polyphenols.

A high oxidative stress buffering effect that is relevant to pollution and smoke exposure was observed in smokers who consumed 300 millilitres of carrot juice per day. This resulted in an increase in plasma antioxidants and a reduction in lymphocyte DNA damage.

Blends of apple, citrus, and berry juices that are rich in polyphenols from fruit: A meta-analysis of healthy adults found that higher intakes of polyphenols derived from fruit were related with improved lung function. This finding suggests that polyphenol-forward juices can supplement the consumption of whole foods when fiber intake is appropriate.

2. Who can Drink:

- Using targeted timing for performance (for example, pre-rehabilitation beetroot juice) and daily consistency for anti-inflammatory benefits, all of the juices above can be included into a pattern that is related with superior respiratory metrics. This pattern is based on the Mediterranean diet and the DASH diet.
- For children (school-aged and teenagers), a diet that is high in fiber and that controls airway inflammation through gut–lung communication can be supplemented with small portions of vegetable and polyphenol-forward juices. However, it is important to remember that whole meals should continue to be the primary source of nutrition.

3. What dosage should I take:

Beetroot juice: In clinical protocols, 140 milliliters of nitrate-rich beetroot juice was administered around two to three hours prior to exercise or rehabilitation. A multi-week course of treatment during rehabilitation also improved walking tests and daily steps in patients with chronic obstructive pulmonary disease (COPD).

Protocols that administered approximately 45 milligrams of lycopene per day through tomato juice were found to reduce airway inflammation parameters in persons who suffer from asthma over a period of seven days. It is possible to implement comparable daily intakes in practical situations.

To improve asthma symptoms and some lung function indices, human trials used pomegranate extract (capsules) at a dosage of 500 milligrams per day for a period of eight weeks. When consumed as juice, begin with 120–240 milliliters per day alongside meals to acquire polyphenols within a balanced diet.

To boost antioxidant status and prevent DNA damage in smokers, a population that is under high oxidative stress relevant to lung health, drinking 300 milliliters of carrot juice every day for eight weeks was found to be effective.

Polyphenol-forward blends: Consuming 180–240 milliliters per day of apple, citrus, or berry-based juices might increase the amount of polyphenols that are associated with improved lung function. This should be done in conjunction with meals that are high in fiber in order to complement the gut–lung axis.

4. Who ought to be avoided or restricted:

The juice of grapefruit: CYP3A4 suppression, which can cause drug levels to rise after as little as around 200 milliliters, should be avoided when taking several medications, including some statins, calcium channel blockers, and immunosuppressants. It is recommended to discuss potential interactions with a clinician or pharmacist.

Juices with a high sugar conte: If not you are trying to manage your weight or your cardiometabolic risk, you should choose options that are vegetable-forward or diluted. This is because the most significant lung advantages come from overall dietary patterns (Mediterranean/DASH) rather than sugar-dense liquids.

Individual sensitivities: The acidity of tomatoes and citrus fruits can cause reflux in some people; therefore, it is important to modify your selections while maintaining the advantages of polyphenols and lycopene through food-based alternatives, if necessary.

5. Some suggestions for achieving a balanced energy:

In conjunction with meals: To match with Mediterranean and DASH patterns, which are linked to improved respiratory outcomes and to moderate glycemic load, juices should be consumed in conjunction with meals that highlight vegetables, legumes, whole grains, nuts, and olive oil.

In order to take advantage of the nitrate-related endurance improvements that are noticed when timed prior to activity, it is recommended that beetroot juice be consumed before to pulmonary rehabilitation or planned walks.

6. Expected advantages to get:

- Endurance and the economy of oxygen both: Nitrate-rich beetroot has the potential to increase plasma nitrate and nitrite levels, as well as improve functional walking or shuttle-walk endurance in patients with COPD when timed or coupled with rehabilitation.

- Airway inflammation control: Lycopene-rich tomato juice reduced neutrophilic airway inflammation and improved clinical asthma parameters in controlled trials.

- In asthma, pomegranate extract was found to be effective in reducing the frequency of dyspnea and activity limitation, along with bringing about favorable changes in inflammatory markers. Pomegranate juice, on the other hand, provides similar polyphenols and is a food-first choice.
- Oxidative stress buffering: Carrot juice boosted circulating antioxidants and decreased lymphocyte DNA damage in smokers, which supported resilience against oxidative loads associated to smoke and pollutants caused by smoking
- Support for polyphenols: A higher intake of polyphenols generated from fruit is associated with improved lung function in healthy individuals, which in turn reinforces the role that polyphenol-forward juices play as supplements to diets consisting of whole foods.

7. Best time to drink:

- Modes of stability: Juices that are high in polyphenols and vegetable-forward should be incorporated into daily routines of the Mediterranean and DASH diets, which are associated with improved lung metrics and symptom profiles.

- To maximize the endurance gains shown in COPD walking and shuttle tests when timed pre-exercise, it is recommended to consume nitrate-rich beets around two to three hours prior to any planned activity or rehabilitation.

By prioritizing beetroot, tomato, pomegranate, carrot, and polyphenol-forward blends—and using them consistently with meals and strategically before activity—juices can meaningfully complement whole-food dietary patterns that support lung function, exercise capacity, and inflammation control.

Chapter 10

Most Effective workouts for Healthy Lung

By combining regular aerobic activity, muscle strengthening, and targeted breathing or inspiratory muscle training with interval formats and pulmonary rehabilitation, the most effective exercises for lung health are those that yield the largest and fastest gains in capacity, symptoms, and quality of life across a wide range of conditions and ages. In order to optimize the advantages and ensure the safety of both adults and children, it is important to combine them with intelligent warm-ups, airway clearance when mucus is an issue, and timing that considers the environment.

1. Aerobic workouts for the core:

Start with ten to fifteen minutes of brisk walking or walking on a treadmill, and gradually increase your time until you are walking for twenty to thirty minutes on most days. Both continuous and interval formats improve exercise capacity and dyspnea in patients with chronic pulmonary disease.

Interval training is at least as effective as continuous training and can modestly reduce exercise-induced dyspnea, but differences are frequently below clinical thresholds.

Cycling (either upright or recumbent): Alternate between moderate efforts for one to three minutes with easy pedaling.

Swimming or water walking is a gentle form of conditioning that works the entire body and reduces the stress on the joints.

To manage symptoms while accumulating time, it is recommended to employ timed breathing and rest at the pool's edge.

2. Proven methods of breathing exercises:

Exhalation through the diaphragm: With one hand on the chest and the other on the abdomen, inhale through the nose to "lift" the abdomen, and exhale slowly. Practice this technique for five to ten minutes every day, as well as during cool-downs, to reduce the amount of effort required to breathe.

By inhaling through the nose for two counts and exhaling through the pursed lips for four counts, patients with chronic obstructive pulmonary disease (COPD) can reduce their respiratory rate and dynamic hyperinflation, so making it easier to tolerate exertion when walking or climbing stairs.

3. Conditioning of the respiratory muscles:

Resistance training for the inspiratory muscles (IMT) using a threshold device: More than three sessions per week, for ten to twenty minutes each, at a pressure that is less than sixty percent of the maximal inspiratory pressure, improves inspiratory strength, dyspnea, and quality of life in COPD patients; cycles of six to twelve weeks should be considered, and loads should be reevaluated.

Those individuals who have been diagnosed with inspiratory weakness are the ones who benefit the most from including IMT into comprehensive pulmonary rehabilitation; the design of the program should be tailored to individualize both intensity and progression.

4. Both strength and movement are essential:

Two to three days a week of light resistance training: Exercises such as chair stands, wall push-ups, band rows, and calf raises are essential components of pulmonary rehabilitation regimens because they help support posture and ventilatory mechanics.

When performing mobility exercises, do some gentle thoracic rotations and shoulder openers before walking or cycling. This will increase the comfort of the chest wall and the adherence to the breathing rhythm.

5. How often and for how long:

Aim to be active on most days: Start with bouts of ten to fifteen minutes and work your way up to twenty to thirty minutes for a total weekly habit that is suitable for symptoms and recovery, with consistency being prioritized over intensity at the beginning.

Both interval and continuous training are helpful: However, brief intervals (for example, one to three minutes of exertion followed by one to three minutes of easy) might assist lessen the sensation of being out of breath and collect more overall work early in the training process.

Increasing one variable at a time to time, then frequency, and finally intensity—is the progression that should be followed to preserve adherence and symptom control within the framework of pulmonary rehabilitation principles.

6. Ideal times to carry them out:

The temperature and the quality of the air: Sessions should be scheduled outside on days when the local air quality is better and temperatures are warmer to reduce the amount of pollutants and cold-air bronchospasm triggers. On days with high pollution levels, sessions should be rescheduled or moved indoors.

Time management that considers symptoms involves selecting times of the day when symptoms are typically at their lowest and medications (such as bronchodilators) are "on board" if they have been prescribed. During activity, pursed-lip breathing should be utilized as required.

7. Add-ons:

On the days of rehabilitation, the nitrate strategy: It is recommended to explore pre-session nutrition that improves endurance, such as nitrate sources, in conjunction with training. Clinical research have shown that combining training with such tactics has improved walking performance in patients with chronic obstructive pulmonary disease (COPD).

Combining education with training: A comprehensive pulmonary rehabilitation program, which includes exercise training, education, and self-management, is a suggested standard for chronic respiratory disease. This program improves the distance that can be walked in six minutes and reduces dyspnoea.

8. Safety and Practical Tips:

To stabilize breathing and heart rate, perform a warm-up and cool-down consisting of five minutes of easy pace before and after the workout. During the cool-down, use diaphragmatic and pursed-lip breathing techniques.

In order to safely accumulate total time, it is recommended to pause and recover with pursed-lip breathing when the level of breathlessness reaches "moderate." After that, restart intervals to accumulate total time.

Environment: On days with a low air quality index (AQI), it is best to opt for cleaner indoor air or well-ventilated rooms; check the local AQI and try to avoid peak traffic hours wherever feasible.

9. Model of a weekly schedule

- ❑ Monday: A brisk walk for twenty minutes in a continuous manner, followed by a five-minute diaphragmatic or pursed-lip cool-down.

- Tuesday: Bands circuit on Tuesday 20 minutes of upper, lower, and core exercises, with ten minutes of diaphragmatic practices.

- Wednesday: Bike intervals on Wednesday 5 minutes of moderate activity followed by 2 minutes of easy activity, followed by 5 minutes of cool-down.

- Thursday: Restorative mobility and ten minutes of diaphragmatic breathing are scheduled for this day.
- Friday: On Friday, perform brisk walk intervals consisting of six minutes of brisk walking followed by two minutes of easy walking, with pursed-lip breathing in between each interval.

- Saturday: Strength circuit for twenty minutes and a brisk stroll for ten minutes on Saturday.

- Sunday: A gentle swim or nature stroll for twenty to thirty minutes, with timed breathing during the entire activity.

The exercises and routines that have been named are in accordance with the principles of pulmonary rehabilitation. They include the reduction of breathlessness during activity, the development of endurance and confidence, and the ability to accommodate day-to-day variations in symptoms and improvements in air quality.

Chapter 11

Manifestation:

The meaning of the phrase "effective manifestation" In actuality, manifestation is not a form of magical thinking but rather a collection of cognitive and behavioural tactics that establish a connection between a desired outcome and particular barriers and actions that are based on cues. This increases the likelihood that goals will be acted upon in a consistent manner.

Manifestation for a Healthy Lung:

Here is given a compilation of a set of morning and bedtime lung-health manifestation charts combining wellness-based and spiritual affirmations. They'll be the statements with an inspirational, clinical, and meditative tone, tailored for your healthy lungs.

Healthy Lung Manifestations (Morning & Bedtime): Combining evidence-based wellness with uplifting affirmations can support lung health. Guided breathwork and mindful habits strengthen the lungs. Studies show daily breathing exercises improve mood and may even boost lung function, while deep inhalations increase alertness. The following example phrases (short and longer, energetic morning vs. calming bedtime) blend inspirational and meditative tones for US readers, reinforcing healthy breathing habits.

Morning Lung Manifestations (Energizing):

Breathing affirmations in the morning focus on energy, oxygenation, and vitality. They reinforce habits like deep inhalations, physical activity, and mindful breathing that improve lung function.

- "I inhale deeply and energize my body with every breath." This deep morning breath fills my lungs with oxygen and increases alertness, kick-starting my day with strength.
- "My lungs are strong and resilient, powering me through this day." I focus on my lungs working healthily, reflecting that breathing training can improve lung function.
- "I move and breathe with confidence." Regular activity and mindful breathing keep my lungs fit.
- "I welcome fresh air into my life." Visualizing fresh air and energy aligns with evidence that slow, conscious breathing supports heart and lung health.
- "I strengthen my lungs with each breath." My daily habits – exercise, fresh air, and mindful breathing – support lung health.

Bedtime Lung Manifestations (Calming):

Before sleep, affirmations can promote relaxation and healing. Slow, controlled breathing reduces stress and prepares the body for rest.

- "With every slow exhale, I release tension and relax." Exhaling fully engages the diaphragm and calms the nervous system, helping to reduce stress.
- "I am grateful for my healthy, healing lungs." Gratitude and positive focus can improve well-being, which supports my lung health.
- "I trust my body to heal as I sleep." This mindset pairs with evidence that mindfulness and breathwork can improve lung function and reduce anxiety.
- "I breathe in calm and breathe out strength." Each slow breath slows my heart rate and eases my mind, backed by studies of breathwork in stress reduction.

"Each breath restores my lungs and eases my mind." Emphasizing restful breathing helps buffer stress and promote lung recovery during sleep.

Chapter 12

Daily Habits: Foundations for Lifelong Health and Performance

Effective daily habits go further than ordinary routines; they can be understood as potent biological instruments that regulate hormones, enhance energy levels, and synchronize mental and physical functions for sustained health. These five habits activate crucial physiological pathways that promote mental clarity, emotional resilience, metabolic equilibrium, and enduring cognitive health. Their impact extends beyond productivity; they also foster health, avert disease, and unleash human potential.

1. Prioritizing Consistent, High-Quality Sleep

Hormonal Regulation and Cognitive Function:

Sleep is the primary regulator of neuroendocrine equilibrium and cellular restoration. During deep sleep, the brain does synaptic pruning, clears metabolic waste (like beta-amyloid) through the glymphatic system, and strengthens memory traces. During slow-wave sleep, the body releases the most growth hormone, which speeds up the repair of tissues and the making of proteins. REM sleep helps with problem-solving, emotional integration, and creative thinking.

Regular sleep-wake cycles help the body stay in sync with its 24-hour rhythm,

which helps the body release cortisol in the morning and melatonin at night. Not getting enough sleep messes up leptin and ghrelin, which makes you hungrier and more likely to gain weight. It also makes insulin less effective and makes it harder for your body to break down glucose and melatonin at night. Not getting enough sleep messes up leptin and ghrelin, which makes you hungrier and more likely to gain weight. It also makes insulin less effective and makes it harder for your body to break down glucose.

Long-Term Systemic Benefits:

- Neuroprotection: Maintains hippocampal volume and reduces risk for neurodegeneration.
- Endocrine Balance: Stabilizes adrenal output and thyroid function.
    - Immune Resilience: Enhances T-cell activity and natural killer cell response
    - Metabolic Health: Improves mitochondrial efficiency and glucose control.

2. Engaging in Daily Physical Activity

Mitochondrial Biogenesis and Cardiovascular Health:

Regular exercise boosts cardiac output, skeletal muscle glucose uptake, and oxygen consumption (VO_2) through pathways that don't depend on insulin. Exercise activates the PGC-1α and AMPK pathways, which leads to the creation of new mitochondria and better aerobic capacity. Resistance training turns on mTOR signaling, which helps muscles grow and makes proteins, both of which are important for keeping lean mass and a high metabolic rate as you get older.

Exercise also helps the brain make new blood vessels and neurons, especially in the hippocampus, which helps with learning and controlling emotions. Even moderate daily activity, like brisk walking, can greatly lower the risk of death from any cause by making the heart work better and the blood vessels more flexible.

Long-Term Systemic Benefits:

- Cardiovascular: Reduces resting heart rate, blood pressure, and arterial stiffness.
- Cognitive: Increases BDNF, supporting neuroplasticity and cognitive reserve.
- Emotional: Elevates endorphins, serotonin, and dopamine to reduce stress and depression.
- Longevity: Associated with longer telomeres and decreased biological aging.

3. Practicing Conscious Breathing

Autonomic Regulation and Oxygen Efficiency:

Breathing is one of the few automatic functions that can be controlled on purpose, which means you can control the autonomic nervous system on purpose. Breathing techniques like diaphragmatic breathing, box breathing, and alternate nostril breathing (nadi shodhana) lower sympathetic activity (fight or flight) and boost the parasympathetic system (rest and digest). This makes vagal tone and heart rate variability (HRV) better.

Deep, slow breathing makes alveolar ventilation better, helps the body handle more carbon dioxide, and helps gas exchange work better. More nitric oxide is made when you breathe through your nose, which opens up blood vessels and helps oxygen get to peripheral tissues. It also helps mitochondria use oxygen better and lowers oxidative stress.

Long-Term Systemic Benefits:

- Nervous System: Reduces cortisol and adrenaline levels; supports calm and focus.
- Respiratory Health: Expands lung capacity and respiratory muscle efficiency.
- Mental Health: Decreases anxiety, promotes emotional regulation and resilience.
- Cellular Metabolism: Improves ATP production and reduces reactive oxygen species (ROS).

4. Staying Hydrated and Eating Nutrient-Dense Foods

Cellular Integrity and Metabolic Optimization:

Water is the medium for all biochemical reactions and is needed for thermoregulation, moving nutrients, and cellular respiration. Even losing 1–2% of your body weight can make it harder to think, make you more tired, and make your aerobic performance worse. Drinking enough water also helps keep the mucosal barrier strong and the lymphatic system working, which is good for the immune system.

When you drink enough water and eat foods high in polyphenols, fiber, omega-3 fatty acids, and antioxidants, they help keep the gut microbiota in balance, lower chronic inflammation, and fuel mitochondrial processes. Oxidative phosphorylation is how cells make energy, and nutrients like magnesium, B-vitamins, and CoQ10 are important cofactors in this process.

Long-Term Systemic Benefits:

- Metabolic: Stabilizes blood sugar and insulin response.
- Digestive: Supports gut flora diversity and nutrient absorption.
- Cognitive: Protects neurons through antioxidant and anti-inflammatory mechanisms.
- Immune: Enhances immune signaling and reduces pro-inflammatory cytokines.

•

5. ***Practicing Daily Reflection or Mindfulness***

Prefrontal Activation and Emotional Regulation:

Intentional reflection—through journaling, meditation, or mindful awareness—fortifies neural circuits associated with emotional regulation, cognitive flexibility, and interoception. Gratitude journaling and mindfulness meditation are two practices that make the prefrontal cortex and anterior cingulate cortex more active. These areas are in charge of planning, focus, and empathy.

These activities lower baseline cortisol levels by lowering the activity of the amygdala, improving executive control, and changing the HPA axis. Over time, regular reflection changes the structure of the brain, making the cortex thicker and improving the connections between the emotional and logical parts of the brain.

Long-Term Systemic Benefits:

- Cognition: Enhances working memory, decision-making, and attention.
- Mental Health: Reduces symptoms of depression, anxiety, and rumination.
- Neuroplasticity: Supports long-term learning and behavior change.
- Resilience: Increases stress tolerance and post-traumatic growth.

Integrated Impact: Habit Synergy

These five habits are very closely related to each other. Sleep helps you recover from exercise and control your emotions. Movement improves the quality of sleep and metabolic health. Breathing helps you stay focused and full of energy. Food gives you energy to move and think. Reflecting on things helps you be more aware of yourself and stick to your habits.

They all:

- Encourage the best connection between the brain and body.
- Lower the risk of chronic disease in all systems.
- Make yourself more adaptable, focused, and purposeful.

- Make life better in both quality and quantity.

Chapter 13

Effective Lunch & Dinner recipes for Healthy lungs

Our lungs are the silent engines of life, working tirelessly every second to deliver oxygen to every cell of our body. Yet, in today's world, they face constant challenges air pollution, smoking, stress, and unhealthy diets can all weaken their ability to function at their best. Scientific research shows that certain nutrients—such as antioxidants, omega-3 fatty acids, vitamins C, E, A, magnesium, and plant flavonoids directly support lung function and help fight oxidative stress. In simple terms, food can either fuel your lungs or burden them.

1. Grilled Salmon with Quinoa & Steamed Broccoli

Bowl = (Quinoa) + (Brocoli) + (Garlic) + (Olive Oil) + (Lemon Juice)

Why this helps the lungs:

- Salmon (Fish): Rich in omega-3 fatty acids, which reduce lung inflammation and improve airflow.
- Quinoa: A magnesium-rich grain that helps relax the bronchial muscles.
- Broccoli: Contains sulforaphane, a compound that supports detoxification in lung tissues.

Ingredients (For 2 people):

- 2 salmon fillets (120–150g each)
- 1 cup quinoa
- 2 cups broccoli florets
- 2 tbsp olive oil
- 1 garlic clove (minced)
- Juice of 1 lemon

- Salt and black pepper to taste

Instructions:

1. Rinse quinoa and cook in 2 cups of water until fluffy.
2. Marinate salmon with olive oil, garlic, lemon juice, salt, and pepper.
3. Grill salmon for 3–4 minutes per side, until golden and flaky.
4. Steam broccoli until bright green (avoid overcooking).
5. Serve salmon over quinoa, with broccoli on the side.

Nutritional Boost: High in protein, omega-3s, antioxidants, and fiber. Supports lung repair and reduces airway inflammation.

2. Lentil & Spinach Soup with Whole Grain Bread

Lentils **Spinach** **Whole grain bread**

Why this helps the lungs:

- Lentils: Provide plant protein, iron, and fiber to support oxygen transport.
- Spinach: Rich in vitamin C, vitamin E, and carotenoids to strengthen lung tissue.
- Soup: Helps thin mucus, keeping airways clear.

Ingredients (For 4 People):

- 1 cup red or green lentils (washed)
- 1 medium onion, chopped
- 2 carrots, diced
- 3 garlic cloves, minced
- 1 tsp cumin
- ½ tsp turmeric
- 6 cups vegetable broth or water
- 2 cups fresh spinach leaves

- 1 tbsp olive oil
- Salt & pepper to taste

Instructions:

1. Heat olive oil in a pot, sauté onion, garlic, and carrots until soft.
2. Add cumin, turmeric, and stir.
3. Add lentils and broth, simmer 25–30 mins until lentils are tender.
4. Stir in spinach at the end and cook for 2 minutes until wilted.
5. Serve hot with whole-grain bread.

Nutritional Boost: High fiber soup that helps reduce systemic inflammation and keeps lungs hydrated.

3. Turmeric-Ginger Chicken with Brown Rice & Green Beans

Bowl = (Chicken Breast) + (Turmeric) + (Brown Rice) + (Beans) + (Ginger) + (Yogurt)

Why this helps the lungs:

- **Chicken**: Lean protein that helps repair damaged lung tissue.
- **Turmeric & Ginger**: Natural anti-inflammatory compounds that support airway health.
- **Green Beans**: Rich in vitamin C and antioxidants to protect against lung damage.

Ingredients (Serves 2):

- 2 chicken breasts (120–150g each)
- 1 cup brown rice
- 2 cups green beans, trimmed
- 1 tsp turmeric powder
- 1 tbsp fresh ginger, grated
- 2 garlic cloves, minced
- 2 tbsp plain yogurt (for marinade)
- 1 tbsp olive oil
- Salt & pepper

Instructions:

1. Mix yogurt, turmeric, ginger, garlic, salt, and pepper. Marinate chicken for at least 30 minutes.
2. Cook brown rice until fluffy.
3. Grill or pan-cook chicken for 4–5 minutes per side until golden.
4. Steam green beans and drizzle with olive oil.
5. Serve chicken over rice with beans on the side.

Nutritional Boost: Combines anti-inflammatory spices with lean protein and fiber, supporting stronger lung function.

4. Stir-Fried Tofu with Mixed Vegetables & Garlic

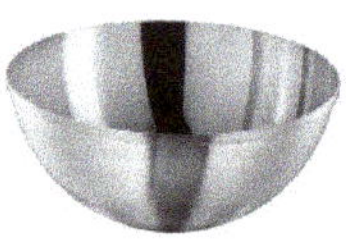 =  +  +  + 

+  + 

***Bowl* = (Tofu) + (Red Bell pepper) + (Carrot) + (Zucchini) + (Garlic) + (Spinach)**

Why this helps the lungs:

- **Tofu**: Provides plant protein and calcium for lung tissue repair.
- **Garlic**: Known for improving lung capacity and reducing respiratory infections.
- **Colorful vegetables**: High in beta-carotene, vitamin C, and flavonoids that keep lungs strong.

Ingredients (For 3 People):

- 250g firm tofu, cubed
- 1 red bell pepper, sliced
- 1 carrot, thinly sliced
- 1 zucchini, sliced
- 1 cup spinach
- 3 garlic cloves, minced
- 2 tbsp olive or sesame oil
- 2 tbsp low-sodium soy sauce
- 1 tsp sesame seeds (optional)

Instructions:

1. Heat oil in a wok, sauté garlic until fragrant.
2. Add tofu cubes and fry until lightly golden.
3. Add vegetables (bell pepper, carrot, zucchini), stir-fry 3–4 minutes.
4. Toss in spinach, soy sauce, and sesame seeds. Stir briefly and serve hot.

Nutritional Boost: A rainbow of vegetables delivers antioxidants that fight oxidative stress in lungs.

5. Baked Sweet Potato with Black Bean & Avocado Salad

Bowl = (Sweet Potato) + (Black Beans) + (Avacado) + (Tomato) + (Cilantro) (Lime)

Why this helps the lungs:

- Sweet Potato: Packed with beta-carotene (vitamin A precursor) to maintain the lung lining.
- Black Beans: Provide protein and fiber for energy and gut-lung connection.
- Avocado: Rich in vitamin E and healthy fats to reduce inflammation in lung tissues.

Ingredients (For 2 People):

- 2 medium sweet potatoes
- 1 cup cooked black beans
- 1 ripe avocado, diced
- 1 small tomato, chopped
- 2 tbsp cilantro, chopped
- Juice of 1 lime
- Salt & pepper

Instructions:

1. Bake sweet potatoes at 200°C (400°F) for 35–40 minutes until tender.
2. In a bowl, mix black beans, avocado, tomato, cilantro, lime juice, salt & pepper.
3. Slice baked sweet potato and top with the bean-avocado salad.

Nutritional Boost: Provides vitamin A, C, E, and fiber, improving immunity and supporting clear airways.

The ingredients we choose vibrant vegetables, antioxidant-rich fruits, lean proteins, legumes, whole grains, healing spices, and healthy fats work together like nature's medicine. By making these meals part of your routine, you're not only strengthening your lungs, but also improving your overall energy, mood, and longevity.

Remember, healthy lungs don't just come from food alone. Pair these recipes with mindful habits like **deep breathing exercises, regular physical activity, proper hydration, and minimizing exposure to toxins** for the best results.

Chapter 14

Breathing Better with Indoor Plants

Every breath we take depends on the quality of the air around us. While outdoor pollution is a growing concern, many people don't realize that indoor air can often be more polluted than outdoor air. Dust, mold, cleaning chemicals, cigarette smoke, and toxins released from furniture and paints (known as volatile organic compounds, or VOCs) can silently affect our lung health every single day. The good news? Nature has given us a simple, beautiful, and effective solution indoor plants. Beyond their calming presence, certain plants act as natural air purifiers, absorbing harmful toxins, releasing fresh oxygen, and even balancing indoor humidity. Scientific studies, including NASA's Clean Air Study, have proven that houseplants can significantly reduce indoor air pollutants and improve overall respiratory wellness.

For people with asthma, allergies, or weak lungs, keeping the right plants indoors can be life-changing. These plants don't just decorate your home they actively create a cleaner, fresher, and lung-friendly environment.

1. Aloe Vera (Aloe Barbadensis Miller)

Why it helps the lungs:

Aloe vera is not just a skin-soothing plant, it's also a powerful natural air purifier. It absorbs harmful chemicals like **formaldehyde** and **benzene** (commonly found in paints, cleaning products, and plastics). Aloe also increases oxygen levels during the night, making it a great plant for bedrooms. More oxygen means easier breathing and healthier lungs.

Health Benefits:

- Improves air quality by removing toxins.
- Supports better sleep with increased oxygen.
- Reduces the burden on lungs caused by indoor pollutants.

Care Instructions:

- Needs bright, indirect sunlight.
- Water only when the soil is dry (every 2–3 weeks).
- Perfect for windowsills or bedrooms.

Noted: The gel inside aloe leaves is rich in vitamins and antioxidants, useful for skin and digestion, so it's a true multi-purpose plant.

2. ***Areca Palm (Dypsis Lutescens)***

Why it helps the lungs:

Known as one of the best natural humidifiers, the Areca Palm releases plenty of water vapor into the air. This keeps the indoor environment moist, which is crucial for people suffering from asthma, dry cough, or sinus issues. Dry air often irritates airways, while humid air helps lungs stay clear and comfortable.

Health Benefits:

- Increases indoor humidity naturally.
- Removes toxins like **xylene** and **toluene** from the air.
- Reduces throat irritation, cough, and dryness.

Care Instructions:

- Keep in bright, indirect sunlight.
- Water regularly, but don't let the roots sit in standing water.
- Mist the leaves occasionally to keep them fresh.

Noted: This plant can grow tall and bushy, so it doubles as a natural décor piece while protecting your lungs.

3. Snake Plant (Sansevieria trifasciata)

Why it helps the lungs:
Popularly called the **"bedroom plant,"** the snake plant is unique because it continues releasing oxygen even at night (most plants release oxygen only during the day). This supports better sleep and oxygen flow while you rest. It also filters harmful chemicals like **benzene, trichloroethylene, and formaldehyde**, which can damage the lungs over time.

Health Benefits:

- Improves nighttime oxygen levels.
- Filters toxic chemicals from indoor air.
- Supports deeper, healthier breathing during sleep.

Care Instructions:

- Thrives in low light, making it very easy to maintain.
- Water sparingly—only once every 2–3 weeks.
- Can survive neglect, making it ideal for beginners.

Noted: Also known as "Mother-in-Law's Tongue," this plant is extremely resilient great for busy people who forget to water regularly.

4. Peace Lily (Spathiphyllum)

Why it helps the lungs:
The Peace Lily is an elegant plant that removes mold spores from the air, making it excellent for people with asthma or allergies. It also filters toxins like benzene, xylene, and formaldehyde. By keeping the air free of allergens and pollutants, it creates a lung-friendly indoor environment.

Health Benefits:

- Cleans mold spores and prevents respiratory irritation.
- Improves indoor air quality by absorbing VOCs (volatile organic compounds).
- Helps reduce the triggers of asthma and allergies.

Care Instructions:

- Prefers shade or low light.
- Keep the soil moist, but don't overwater.
- Wipe leaves occasionally to keep them dust-free.

Noted: Its beautiful white flowers also add a calming, peaceful vibe to the home—perfect for both lung health and mental well-being.

5. Rubber Plant (Ficus elastica)

Why it helps the lungs:

The Rubber Plant is excellent at removing formaldehyde and carbon monoxide—two pollutants that can harm the respiratory system. Its broad leaves are also very effective at trapping dust and allergens, making the air cleaner and lighter for your lungs.

Health Benefits:

- Removes common indoor pollutants that stress the lungs.
- Traps dust and allergens from the air.
- Helps prevent breathing difficulties caused by poor indoor air quality.

Care Instructions:

- Needs bright, filtered light (avoid direct harsh sunlight).
- Water moderately, allowing the topsoil to dry before rewatering.
- Wipe the large leaves to keep them dust-free and effective.

Noted: This plant grows tall and bold, so it can be both a statement piece and a natural air purifier in your living space.

Our lungs work tirelessly to keep us alive, but in today's world, they face constant challenges from polluted air, dust, smoke, and hidden household toxins. While we can't always control the air outside, we can take powerful steps to improve the air inside our homes. Indoor plants are more than decorations; they are **living air filters and natural healers**. Aloe Vera boosts oxygen at night, Areca Palm humidifies the air, Snake Plant supports restful breathing, Peace Lily fights mold and allergens, and the Rubber Plant clears out toxins and dust. Together, these green companions create a cleaner, fresher, and lung-friendly environment.

By combining lung-nourishing foods with air-purifying plants, you create a powerful lifestyle of healing one that protects your respiratory system, boosts immunity, and enhances overall vitality.

Chapter 15

Supplements as Extra Support for Healthy Lungs

Food is the foundation of good health, but sometimes our bodies need a little extra help. Modern lifestyles, stress, poor diets, pollution, and even natural aging can make it difficult to get all the essential nutrients we need for strong, healthy lungs. This is where **supplements** come in acting as reliable allies that fill nutritional gaps and provide targeted support for the respiratory system. Supplements are not a replacement for whole foods, but rather a way to **boost the body's defenses and healing capacity**. Scientific studies have shown that certain nutrients, when taken in the right amounts—can reduce lung inflammation, strengthen immunity, improve oxygen flow, and even protect against long-term damage from smoking or pollution.

Omega-3 Fatty Acids (Fish Oil or Algal Oil)

Why it helps the lungs:

Omega-3 fatty acids are essential fats with powerful **anti-inflammatory properties**. Inflammation is a major factor in lung diseases like asthma, bronchitis, and COPD. By lowering inflammation, omega-3s improve airflow and reduce symptoms such as wheezing or chest tightness. They also support overall cardiovascular health, which benefits oxygen transport throughout the body.

Health Benefits:

- Reduces airway inflammation.
- Improves lung function in people with asthma and COPD.
- Supports immune response against respiratory infections.
- Enhances oxygen delivery by improving blood circulation.

Suggested Dosage:

- 1,000–2,000 mg per day of EPA + DHA combined.
- Best taken with meals for absorption.

Natural Food Sources: Fatty fish (salmon, mackerel, sardines), chia seeds, flaxseeds, walnuts.

Note: For vegetarians/vegans, **algal oil supplements** are an excellent plant-based alternative.

Fish oil supplements may interact with certain medications or supplements. Do not take them without your doctor's approval if you are on any medications (especially blood thinning drugs) or have chronic health conditions such as diabetes, heart disease, kidney disease, liver disease, or any disorder of the pancreas.

Vitamin C

Why it helps the lungs:

Vitamin C is one of the most important antioxidants for respiratory health. It protects lung tissues from **oxidative stress** caused by pollution, smoking, or infections. It also helps the body produce collagen, keeping lung tissue strong and flexible. In people with asthma or frequent colds, vitamin C has been shown to reduce the severity of symptoms.

Health Benefits:

- Neutralizes harmful free radicals in the lungs.
- Strengthens immunity, reducing respiratory infections.
- Improves lung tissue repair and elasticity.
- Supports iron absorption, which boosts oxygen transport.

Suggested Dosage:

- 500–1,000 mg per day.
- Water-soluble, so daily intake is important (excess is flushed out).

Natural Food Sources: Oranges, kiwi, bell peppers, broccoli, strawberries, guava.

Note: Smokers and people exposed to pollution may need **higher vitamin C intake** due to faster depletion.

People with G6PD deficiency, hemochromatosis (iron overload), certain kidney problems, or who are getting certain types of cancer treatment should not take large doses or regular vitamin C supplements. People with diabetes or a history of kidney stones or oxalate nephropathy should also be careful.

Vitamin D

Why it helps the lungs:
Vitamin D isn't just for bones—it's vital for the immune system and lung function. Deficiency has been linked with increased risk of asthma, chronic lung diseases, and frequent respiratory infections. Vitamin D helps regulate immune cell activity, reducing unnecessary inflammation in the airways.

Health Benefits:

- Reduces the risk of asthma attacks and COPD flare-ups.
- Supports immune defense against respiratory infections.
- Helps control airway inflammation.
- Improves lung function in people with vitamin D deficiency.

Suggested Dosage:

- 1,000–2,000 IU per day (sometimes more if blood levels are low, but only under medical supervision).

Natural Sources: Sunlight exposure, fatty fish, fortified milk, eggs.

Note: Many people are deficient due to indoor lifestyles—so supplementation can be crucial for lung health.

People shouldn't usually take a lot of vitamin D, especially who have kidney difficulties, like kidney failure, or who have ever had kidney stones.

N-Acetyl Cysteine (NAC)

Why it helps the lungs:
NAC is a powerful supplement derived from the amino acid **cysteine**. It's best known for boosting **glutathione**, the body's master antioxidant, which protects lung tissue from damage. NAC also works as a **mucolytic**, thinning thick mucus and making it easier to clear from the airways. This makes it especially useful for people with chronic bronchitis, asthma, or COPD.

Health Benefits:

- Breaks down and clears mucus in the lungs.
- Increases glutathione levels, reducing oxidative damage.

- Protects against lung injury from smoking or pollution.
- May reduce the frequency of flare-ups in chronic lung diseases.

Suggested Dosage:

- 600–1,200 mg per day, usually in divided doses.

Natural Sources: Found in high-protein foods like chicken, turkey, yogurt, sunflower seeds, and legumes (but supplement form is more effective for therapeutic use).

Extra Note: NAC has been used in hospitals for decades to treat lung conditions and even acetaminophen overdose—it's that powerful.

Talk to your doctor about which supplements are best for you. NAC may not be safe for persons who: bleed easily, have cystinuria, or take nitroglycerin.

Magnesium

Why it helps the lungs:

Magnesium is a mineral that plays a vital role in **muscle relaxation**, including the muscles in the airways. It acts as a **natural bronchodilator**, helping widen the airways and making it easier to breathe. People with asthma often benefit from higher magnesium intake, and deficiency can worsen respiratory symptoms.

Health Benefits:

- Relaxes airway muscles, improving airflow.
- Reduces the risk of asthma attacks.
- Supports energy production for stronger breathing muscles.
- Balances inflammation in the lungs.

Suggested Dosage:

- 200–400 mg per day.
- Magnesium citrate or glycinate forms are easiest to absorb.

Natural Food Sources: Dark leafy greens, nuts, seeds, whole grains, legumes.

Note: In emergency rooms, IV magnesium is sometimes given for severe asthma attacks—showing how powerful this mineral is for the lungs.

Healthy lungs are essential for a vibrant life, yet they are constantly exposed to stress from pollution, infections, and daily wear and tear. While a nutrient-rich diet is always the first line of defense, supplements can provide targeted support when the body needs an extra boost.

Think of supplements as your outsourced allies: silent helpers that fill the nutritional gaps and make breathing easier, one dose at a time. With the right choices, every inhale can feel lighter, fresher, and more empowering.

People with diabetes, intestinal disease, heart disease, or renal disease should not take magnesium unless their doctor tells them to. Too much If you take too much magnesium, you may feel sick, have diarrhea, have low blood pressure, feel weak, or be tired.

Warning: Talk to your doctor first. Talk to a certified healthcare professional before starting any supplement regimen, especially if you are pregnant, breastfeeding, or already have health problems. This is especially important for those who have asthma, COPD, or other long-term disorders that affect their breathing.

Glossary

Alveoli

Alveoli are millions of tiny, balloon-like air sacs located deep inside the lungs. Their main job is to transfer oxygen from the air you breathe into your bloodstream and remove carbon dioxide from the blood. Because alveoli have very thin walls and are surrounded by blood vessels, they allow gases to pass quickly and efficiently. Healthy alveoli are essential for good energy levels and clear breathing.

Alveolar Ducts

Alveolar ducts are small air passages that lead air from the respiratory bronchioles into clusters of alveoli. Think of them as short hallways that guide air to the exact spots where oxygen exchange happens. If these ducts become inflamed or damaged, breathing efficiency can decrease.

Antioxidants

Antioxidants are protective substances found in fruits, vegetables, and other foods that help defend the body against cellular damage. They neutralize harmful molecules called free radicals, which are produced by pollution, smoking, stress, and normal metabolism. In the lungs, antioxidants help reduce inflammation and protect delicate tissues from long-term damage.

Asthma

Asthma is a long-term condition where the airways become sensitive and inflamed. This causes the air passages to narrow, making breathing difficult. People with asthma may experience wheezing, coughing, chest tightness, or shortness of breath, especially during exercise or exposure to triggers like dust, cold air, or smoke. Asthma can be managed with lifestyle choices and medical care.

Autonomic Nervous System

The autonomic nervous system controls automatic body functions such as breathing, heart rate, and digestion. It has two main parts: one that activates the body during stress and another that calms the body during rest. Breathing exercises can influence this system, helping reduce stress and improve lung efficiency.

Beta-Carotene

Beta-carotene is a natural pigment found in colorful fruits and vegetables like carrots and sweet potatoes. The body converts it into vitamin A, which helps maintain the lining of the lungs and airways. Adequate beta-carotene intake supports immune defense and helps keep lung tissues strong and healthy.

Biomass Fuel

Biomass fuels include materials such as wood, crop waste, or animal dung that are burned for cooking or heating. When used indoors without proper ventilation, they release smoke and harmful particles that can damage the lungs over time. Long-term exposure is linked to chronic respiratory diseases.

Bronchi

Bronchi are the two large air tubes that branch from the trachea and enter the lungs. They act as main highways for air to travel into each lung before further dividing into smaller passages. Healthy bronchi allow smooth airflow and efficient breathing.

Bronchioles

Bronchioles are smaller branches of the bronchi located deeper inside the lungs. They regulate how much air reaches the alveoli by tightening or relaxing. When bronchioles become inflamed or constricted, breathing can feel tight or labored.

Bronchodilation

Bronchodilation refers to the widening of the airways. This happens naturally during exercise or can be triggered by medications. When airways widen, breathing becomes easier because air can flow freely into the lungs.

Bronchopulmonary Segments

These are small, functionally independent sections of the lungs, each supplied by its own airway and blood vessels. Doctors use these segments to locate infections or damage and sometimes remove affected areas surgically without disturbing the rest of the lung.

Carbon Dioxide (CO_2)

Carbon dioxide is a waste gas produced when the body uses oxygen to create energy. The lungs remove carbon dioxide when you exhale. If the lungs cannot remove it efficiently, fatigue, headaches, and breathing discomfort may occur.

Chronic Obstructive Pulmonary Disease (COPD)

COPD is a progressive lung disease that makes breathing increasingly difficult. It includes conditions such as chronic bronchitis and emphysema. COPD is commonly caused by smoking or long-term exposure to polluted air and leads to coughing, mucus buildup, and breathlessness.

Cilia

Cilia are microscopic, hair-like structures lining the airways. They constantly move back and forth to push mucus, dust, and germs out of the lungs. Healthy cilia are essential for keeping the lungs clean and infection-free.

Compliance (Lung)

Lung compliance describes how easily the lungs expand during inhalation. Lungs with good compliance inflate effortlessly, while stiff lungs require more effort to breathe. Poor compliance is often seen in lung diseases or aging.

Diffusion

Diffusion is the natural movement of gases from an area of higher concentration to lower concentration. In the lungs, diffusion allows oxygen to move into the blood and carbon dioxide to move out, without requiring extra energy.

Diaphragm

The diaphragm is a large, dome-shaped muscle beneath the lungs. When it contracts, it pulls air into the lungs; when it relaxes, air moves out. Strong diaphragm function supports deep, efficient breathing.

Dyspnea

Dyspnea is the medical term for shortness of breath. It can occur during physical exertion or at rest and may signal lung, heart, or anxiety-related conditions.

Elastic Recoil

Elastic recoil is the lungs' ability to return to their original size after inhalation. This natural spring-like action helps push air out during exhalation. Loss of recoil makes breathing tiring and less efficient.

Endurance Training

Endurance training includes activities such as walking, cycling, or swimming that improve heart and lung efficiency. Over time, this type of exercise strengthens respiratory muscles and increases oxygen use.

Environmental Pollutants

These are harmful substances in the air, including smoke, dust, chemicals, and fine particles. Long-term exposure can inflame airways, reduce lung capacity, and increase disease risk.

Free Radicals

Free radicals are unstable molecules that damage cells and tissues. They are produced by pollution, smoking, stress, and even normal breathing. Excess free radicals contribute to aging and chronic lung inflammation.

Forced Expiratory Volume (FEV_1)

FEV_1 measures how much air you can forcefully exhale in one second. Doctors use it to assess lung strength and detect conditions like asthma or COPD.

Forced Vital Capacity (FVC)

FVC is the total amount of air you can forcefully breathe out after taking a deep breath. It helps evaluate overall lung capacity.

Gas Exchange

Gas exchange is the process by which oxygen enters the blood and carbon dioxide leaves it. This occurs in the alveoli and is vital for survival and energy production.

Gastroesophageal Reflux Disease (GERD)

GERD is a digestive condition where stomach acid flows back into the throat. Acid irritation can worsen coughing, asthma, and breathing discomfort.

Gut–Lung Axis

The gut–lung axis refers to the connection between digestive health and lung immunity. A healthy gut microbiome supports better immune responses in the lungs.

Hypoxemia

Hypoxemia occurs when oxygen levels in the blood are lower than normal. It can cause fatigue, confusion, and shortness of breath.

Inspiratory Muscle Training (IMT)

IMT involves exercises that strengthen the muscles used to inhale. Stronger inspiratory muscles reduce breathlessness and improve lung efficiency.

Intercostal Muscles

These muscles sit between the ribs and assist breathing by expanding and contracting the chest.

Lung Capacity

Lung capacity is the maximum amount of air your lungs can hold. Higher capacity supports better endurance and oxygen delivery.

Lung Parenchyma

This refers to the working tissue of the lungs involved in gas exchange. Damage to this tissue reduces oxygen transfer.

Manifestation

In this book, manifestation means using focused intention, positive mindset, and consistent action to support lung health habits—not magical thinking.

Mitochondria

Mitochondria are energy-producing structures inside cells. They use oxygen to create energy, making lung health critical for cellular performance.

Mucociliary Escalator

This is the lung's natural cleaning system, where mucus traps particles and cilia move them out of the airways.

Nitric Oxide (NO)

Nitric oxide helps widen blood vessels and improve oxygen delivery. It is produced naturally during nasal breathing.

Oxidative Stress

Oxidative stress occurs when free radicals overwhelm antioxidants, leading to inflammation and tissue damage.

Pleura

The pleura are thin membranes surrounding the lungs that allow smooth movement during breathing.

Pneumothorax

This is a partial or complete lung collapse caused by trapped air in the chest cavity.

Polyphenols

Polyphenols are plant compounds with strong antioxidant and anti-inflammatory effects that protect lung tissue.

Pulmonary Circulation

Pulmonary circulation moves blood between the heart and lungs to exchange oxygen and carbon dioxide.

Pulmonary Rehabilitation

A structured program combining exercise, education, and breathing techniques to improve lung function and quality of life.

Respiratory Rate

The number of breaths taken per minute, often used as a basic indicator of respiratory health.

Restrictive Lung Disease

Conditions that prevent the lungs from fully expanding, making deep breathing difficult.

Sarcopenia

Loss of muscle mass and strength, often seen in chronic lung disease and aging.

Spirometry

A simple breathing test that measures how well the lungs move air in and out.

Surfactant

A natural substance that keeps alveoli from collapsing during breathing.

Systemic Inflammation

Inflammation affecting the entire body, not just one organ, often worsening lung and heart health.

Tidal Volume

The amount of air inhaled or exhaled during normal, relaxed breathing.

Trachea: The windpipe that carries air from the throat to the lungs.

Ventilation: The movement of air into and out of the lungs.

Vital Capacity: The maximum amount of air expelled after a full inhalation.

VO_2 Max: A measure of how efficiently the body uses oxygen during exercise.

Volatile Organic Compounds (VOCs)

Harmful gases released from household products that can irritate and damage the lungs.

References & Further Reading

This book is informed by established principles of respiratory physiology, nutrition science, exercise science, and preventive health research. Readers interested in deeper academic or clinical exploration may consult standard medical and health resources, including publications from:

- World Health Organization (WHO)
- Centers for Disease Control and Prevention (CDC)
- National Institutes of Health (NIH)
- Peer-reviewed journals in respiratory medicine, exercise physiology, and nutrition science

Scientific understanding continues to evolve. Readers are encouraged to consult qualified healthcare professionals for personalized medical guidance.

Final Note:

Healthy lungs are not built through a single diet, exercise, or technique, but through consistent daily choices. Small improvements in breathing, movement, nutrition, sleep, and environment accumulate over time to produce meaningful changes in energy, resilience, and well-being.

The ideas presented in this book are intended to support awareness and informed decision-making. Sustainable health is a long-term practice shaped by patience, consistency, and balance.

A Small Request

If you found this book helpful, practical, or insightful, consider leaving an honest review on Amazon or any other platform where you found it. Your valuable feedback not only helps others discover the book but also supports the continued development of thoughtful and research-driven work.

Your time and perspective are sincerely appreciated.

About the Author

S S Dhar (**Sujit Sutradhar**), born on **25 June 1998**, is an independent author with an academic background in science and mathematics. He completed his graduation in science and later earned a **Master's degree in Mathematics**, building a strong foundation in logical reasoning, research, and analytical thinking.

He has written **more than 50 books** across diverse niches and categories, including but not limited to **self-help, health and wellness, general psychology, general philosophy, success and inspiration, general science, mathematics, business mindset, and wealth management**. Among these works, **more than ten books have received national and international recognition**.

His writing focuses on presenting structured, research-informed ideas in a clear and accessible manner. Through *Healthy Lungs, Healthy Life*, he aims to help readers understand respiratory health and adopt sustainable lifestyle practices that support long-term well-being.

To Know More: **Please visit**: https://ssdhar.com

www.ingramcontent.com/pod-product-compliance
Ingram Content Group UK Ltd.
Pitfield, Milton Keynes, MK11 3LW, UK
UKHW061546190726
13845UKWH00030B/1054

9 789357 597074